HART PICTURE ARCHIVES

Trades & Professions

Under the General Editorship of

Harold H. Hart

Hart Publishing Company, Inc. ● New York City

ISBN NO. 08055-1214-4 (PAPERBACK 08055-0307-2)
LIBRARY OF CONGRESS CATALOG CARD NO. 77-72890

MANUFACTURED IN THE UNITED STATES OF AMERICA

CONTENTS

HOW TO USE THIS BOOK

TRADES & PROFESSIONS is a collection of over 1,000 pictures of many periods, culled from 87 known sources. These pictures have been subdivided into 53 categories.

All these pictures are in the public domain. They derive from magazines, books, and pictures copyrighted by Hart Publishing Company, now released to the public for general use.

So as not to clutter a caption, the source of the picture is given an abbreviated designation. Full publication data may be found in the *Sources* section, in which all sources are listed in alphabetical order, with the full title of the book or magazine, the publisher, and the date of publication. The *Sources* section commences on page 408.

Captions appear only beneath those pictures which call for clear identification. For example, many pictures in the section on *Iron Workers* are identified by the specific task being performed.

Ninety-five pictures are halftones, and they are designated by a square symbol □ at the end of the caption. These pictures, too, are suitable for reproduction, but the user is alerted to rescreen such a picture or convert it into line. All other pictures can be reproduced directly in line.

The *Index* begins on page 410. All index entries set in full caps represent one of the 53 major groupings in this book.

Accountants

Caricature

Punch

Fifty Years of Soviet Art □

The Accountant's Office, Bank of England. *Leslie's* □

Century

Harper's

Actors & Performers

Performing in a Vsevolod
Meyerhold production.
Plays, Players, & Playwrights

In a Chinese theatre.
Century

Police Gazette

French Ad Art

John Howard Payne as "Young Norval."
Leslie's, Vol. 16

The French stage—strolling players. *Leslie's, Vol. 16*

Charles Keane as King Lear. *Century*

Edwin Forrest as King Lear. *Harper's*

Actors & Performers continued

Police Gazette

Drawing by Grandville. *Petites Misères*

The French theatre of the 14th century. *Leslie's*

M. Got as Briac in
"Une Journée D'Agrippa." *Strand*

Art of the Silhouette

Junius Brutus Booth as "Sir Giles Overreach." *Century*

Police Gazette

Actors & Performers continued

Caruso

Leslie's

Punch

French theatre during the reign of Louis XIII. *Leslie's*

Peking tragedians. *Peoples of the World*

Actors & Performers continued

Fifty Years of Soviet Art

Wandering minstrels at Yokahama. *Good Things*

Presentation of "Mirame," a tragedy by Cardinal Richelieu. *Leslie's*

Punch

Police Gazette

Actors & Performers continued

Leslie's

Punch

Punch

Flowers of Happiness

Century

Fliegende Blätter

Flowers of Happiness

Lustige Blätter

Actors & Performers continued

Good Things

Modern Woodcuts

Fliegende Blätter

Early Advertising Art

Art in 1898 □

French Ad Art

Early Advertising Art

Un Autre Monde

Actors & Performers continued

Catchpenny Prints

Life

The acrobat.
Police Gazette, 1892

Book of Days

Fliegende Blätter

Harper's □

Punch

Police Gazette

Harper's

Lustige Blätter

Actors & Performers continued

Harper's

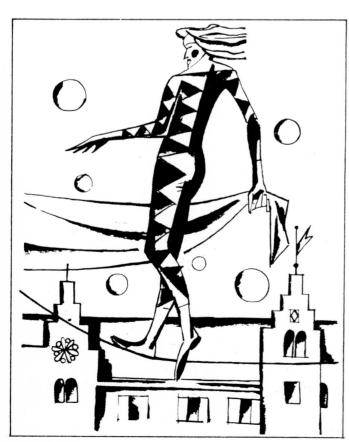

Art of the Book

Punch

Punch

Drawing by Grandville. *Un Autre Monde*

Quaint Cuts

Punch

Actors & Performers continued

Drawing by Grandville. *Un Autre Monde* □

Harper's

Punch

The knife-thrower and his young assistant. *St. Nicholas*

A performing goat. *London Illustrated News*

Pulcinella. *Plays, Players & Playwrights*

Harper's Roundtable

Actors & Performers continued

Leslie's, Vol. 20

Flowers of Happiness

Fliegende Blätter

Art of the Book

Harper's

Punch

Flowers of Happiness □

Agricultural Workers

Spreading husk coffee to dry in the sun. *Leslie's*

Harvesting. *Harper's*

Ploughing rice. *Harper's*

Graphics of Lvov

Old Engravings

Picking coffee beans. *Harper's*

The mower. *Art in 1898*

Agricultural Workers continued

Berry-picking in Central America. *Leslie's*

Early Illustrators

Picture Book of Graphic Arts, Vol. 3

rly Illustrators

Old Engravings

asants gathering seaweed on the French coast. *Leslie's*

Agricultural Workers continued

Graphics of Lvov

Picturesque Palestine

Early Illustrators

Marvels of the New West

Belkin's Stories

Early Illustrators

Haying time. *Tribute Book*

Ancient Egyptians harvesting grapes.
Sunday Book

Agricultural Workers continued

Famous Paintings ☐

Modern Pen Drawing

elkin's Stories

Art of the Book

Agricultural Workers continued

Peasants winnowing grain. *New Woodcuts* □

Harper's, Vol. 75 □

Picking cotton. *History of the United States*

Early Illustrators

Modern Woodcuts

Picking hops. *Harper's*

Agricultural Workers continued

Leslie's

Watering cave-cultured mushrooms. *Leslie's*

Famous Paintings □

Picture Book of Graphic Arts, Vol. 5

Agricultural Workers continued

Hindu method of crop irrigation. *Leslie's*

Art of the Book

Peat-carriers of Scotland. *Peoples of the World*

Turkomen ploughing. *Peoples of the World*

Graphics of Lvov

Old Engravings

English harvesters. *Peoples of the World*

Agricultural Workers continued

Agriculture during the early Iron Age. *Peoples of the World*

Old Engravings

English gleaners. *Peoples of the World*

The Art of the Silhouette

Old Engravings

Harvesting the grapes. *Leslie's*

Agricutlural Workers continued

Threshing corn. *Leslie's*

Art of the Book

Illustrated London News

Scratchboard Drawing

Ploughing with a camel in Egypt. *Harper's* □

Leslie's

Agricultural Workers continued

Drawing by Honoré Daumier. *Daumier Album.* □

Threshing with a sledge. *Sunday Book*

Belkin's Stories

Century Magazine, Vol. 14 □

Harper's

Early Advertising Art

Agricultural Workers continued

Forming cave beds for growing mushrooms. *Leslie's*

Returning from the fields. *Harper's*

Perfect Jewels

Art of the Book

Cutting and hauling sugar cane in Louisiana. *Harper's*

Agricultural Workers continued

Drawing and Design □

Century, Vol. 13

In the vineyard. *Marvels of the New West*

Historians' History

Picture Book of Graphic Arts, Vol. 1

Harvesting grapes for raisins in Fresno. *Century Magazine, Vol. 15* □

Tossing hay. *Harper's* □

Harvesting. *Nikolai Ivanovich Piskarev*

Agricultural Workers continued

Fifty Years of Soviet Art □

Famous Paintings □

Seeding on a bonanza farm. *Marvels of the New West*

Gleaners. *Peoples of the World*

The reaper. *Peoples of the World*

The threshing floor. *Bible Encyclopedia*

Century Magazine, Vol. 15

Agricultural Workers continued

Picture Book of Graphic Arts, Vol. 5

Modern Woodcuts

*Picture Book of
Graphic Arts, Vol. 5*

Agricultural Workers continued

Harvesting on a bonanza farm. *Marvels of the New West*

Ploughing on a bonanza farm. *Marvels of the New West*

Harper's

New Woodcuts

Harvesting in Brittany. *Peoples of the World*

Agricultural Workers continued

Art of the Book □

Modern Woodcuts

Early Illustrators

Hauling sugar cane. *Harper's*

Modern Woodcuts

Agricultural Workers continued

Old Engravings

In the hayfield. *Leslie's*

The colza harvest in Italy. *Leslie's*

Graphics of Lvov

Irrigating an orange grove. *Harper's*

Samoan Islanders picking cotton. *Natural History*

Agricultural Workers continued

Art of the Book

Harper's

New Woodcuts ☐

Graphics of Lvov

Harper's

Harvest time in a California orange grove.
Marvels of the New West

Agricultural Workers continued

Early Illustrators

New Woodcuts □

ew Woodcuts □

king cotton. *Peoples of the World*

Artists

Al'bina Makuraite

Art of the Silhouette

Fifty Years of Soviet Art □

Drawing and Design, No. 4

Artists continued

Harper's

Fliegende Blätter

Modern Pen Drawing

Fifty Years of Soviet Art □

Art of the Book

Art of the Book □

Punch

Artists continued

Harper's

Judge □

Good Things □

Judge □

Century Magazine

Modern Pen Drawing

Artists continued

Drawing by Grandville. *Petites Misères*

Strand □

Drawing and Design, No. 2

Century

Art of the Book

Punch

Good Things

Daumier □

Artists continued

Daumier □

Century

Harper's

Harper's, Vol. 46

Art Of The Book

Judge

Harper's

Artists continued

Aleksandr Vasin

Dictionary of Terms in Art

Harper's

Leslie's, Vol. 16

Punch

The World: Its Cities and Peoples

Drawing by Grandville. *La Vie des Animaux*

Daumier □

Auctioneers

Auctioneer. *Harper's*

Early Advertising Art

Connoisseur

Harper's, Vol. 78

Harper's, Vol. 76

tea auction in New York. *Illustrated London News*

Barbers

Harper's

Semitic barbers. *Picturesque Palestine*

Punch

Harper's

Hindu barber in Madras. *India*

Hairdresser's shop during the reign of Louis XIV. *Leslie's*

Barbers continued

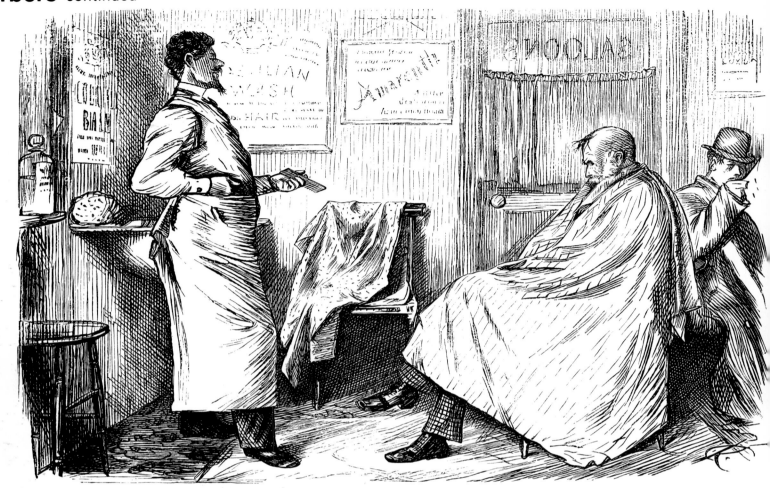

Judge

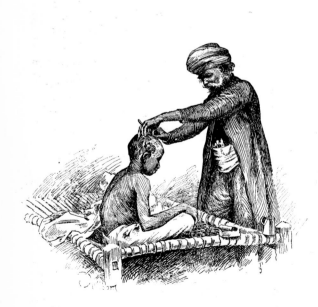

Peoples of the World

Mexican Mustang

abian barber. *Riverside Natural History*

Land and Book

Barbers continued

Turkish barber. *Peoples of the World*

Chinese barber. *Peoples of the World*

Turkish barber. *Leslie's*

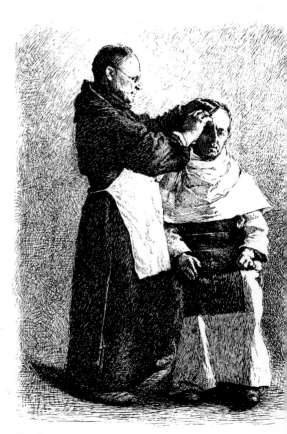

Century

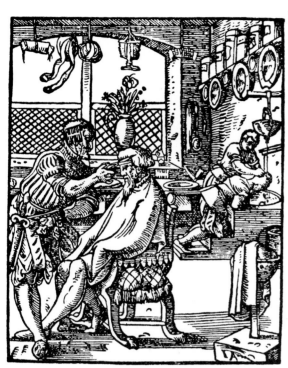

Picture Book of Graphic Arts, Vol. 3

Punch

Natural History of Africa and Asia

Beggars

Harper's

Punch, Vol. 29

Harper's

Mongol beggar. *Through Asia*

That Sister-in-Law of Mine

Lustige Blätter

Droll Stories

Rabelais

Ruthless Rhymes

Century Magazine, Vol. 15

Blacksmiths

Harper's

Picture Book of Graphic Arts, Vol. 3

Harper's

Century Magazine, Vol. 14

dian blacksmith shoeing a bullock. *Illustrated London News*

obert Collyer's blacksmith shop. *Harper's*

Harper's

Blacksmiths continued

Inventing an improved hammer. *Leslie's*

Harper's

Siberian blacksmith. *Century Magazine, Vol. 15*

Book of Days

Century Magazine, Vol. 14

ﬂu blacks mith forging an assegai. *Peoples of the World*

Carpenters

Caricature □

Dutch woodworker. *Leslie's*

Harper's, Vol. 15

...cture Book of Graphic Arts, Vol. 3

Carpenters continued

Picture Book of Graphic Arts, Vol. 3

Fifty Years of Soviet Art □

A carpenter's shop in Galilee. *Century Magazine, Vol. 15*

The village carpenter. *Harper's*

Damascan carpenter steadying his saw with his foot. *Picturesque Palestine*

Ancient Egyptian carpenter with a saw. *Sunday Book*

Picture Book of Graphic Arts, Vol. 3

Ceramicists

Potters at work in Rasheiyet El Fukhar. *Picturesque Palestine*

Porcelain decorators in Tokyo. *House and Home*

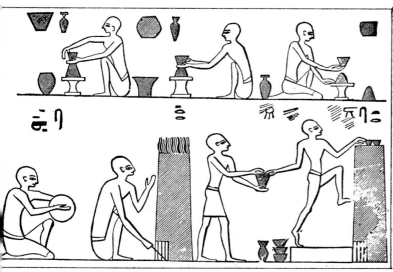

Egyptian potters. *Bible Encyclopedia*

Ancient Greek potter.
Life of Greeks and Romans

Ancient Greek potter.
Life of Greeks and Romans

The potter at his wheel. *Land and Book*

An early potter. *Peoples of the World*

Clergy

Harper's

Russian priest. *Peoples of the World*

A Samoiede priest. *Peoples of the World*

Century

Punch, Vol. 30

yssinian priest and monk. *Peoples of the World*

Bab Ballads

Clergy continued

Rabelais

Masterpieces

The rabbi. *Harper's*

The Archimandrite Nicodemus. *Leslie's*

Lutheran clergyman of Norway. *Leslie's*

Century □

Froissart's Modern Chronicles

Russian minorites. *Peoples of the World*

Harper's Monthly, Vol. 10

Clergy continued

Harper's, Vol. 10

Harper's, Vol. 10

Harper's, Vol. 10

Harper's, Vol. 10

Harper's, Vol. 10

Harper's, Vol. 10

Harper's, Vol. 10

Harper's, Vol. 10

Harper's, Vol. 10

Harper's, Vol. 68

Harper's, Vol. 79

Harper's, Vol. 10

Harper's, Vol. 10

Dictionary of Terms in Art

Clergy continued

New Woodcuts

A Mexican priest going to administer to a dying parishioner. *Leslie's*

Monk tending the sick. *Harper's*

A native priest. *Natural History of Man*

Bab Ballads

Art of the Book ▫

Century Dictionary

The metropolitan of St. Petersburg and his clergy. *Peoples of the World*

Clergy continued

Masterpieces

Droll Stories

Works of Rabelais

A friar of the 8th century.
History of the World

Swiss ecclesiastic of the Middle Ages.
History of the World

Brahmin priest. *Peoples of the World*

The circuit preacher. *Harper's*

Harper's

Clergy continued

Russian priest. *Harper's*

A Jesuit missionary among the Indians. *Harper's*

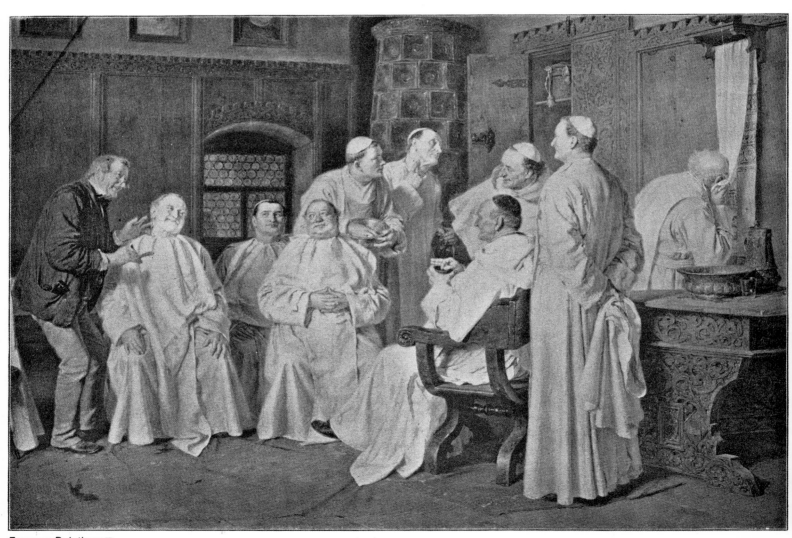

Famous Paintings □

Deutsches Lachen

Masterpieces □

Peruvian priest. *Aldine*

Archbishop of the 8th century.
History of the World

Clergy continued

Cranford

The Dalai-Lama. *Zell's Encyclopedia*

Masterpieces

Caricature

Deutsches Lachen

Century

Century □

Prussian procession. *Harper's* □

Clergy continued

Byzantine priest. *History of the World*

Priest of the Greek Church and peasant woman. *Peoples of the World*

Harper's

Punch

Harper's Monthly, Vol. 10

A Franciscan missionary among the Indians. *Leslie's*

A lama. *Through Asia*

eading room in a monastery. *Strand* □

New Woodcuts □

Clergy continued

The aged monk. *Peoples of the World*

Buddhist priest of Ceylon.
Peoples of the World

Byzantine priest. *History of the World*

High-priest offering incense. *Sunday Book*

Street preacher. *Harper's*

Russian priest. *History of the World*

Russian monk. *Peoples of the World*

Coachmen & Cabbies

English coachman of the "upper ten." *Leslie's*

Harper's

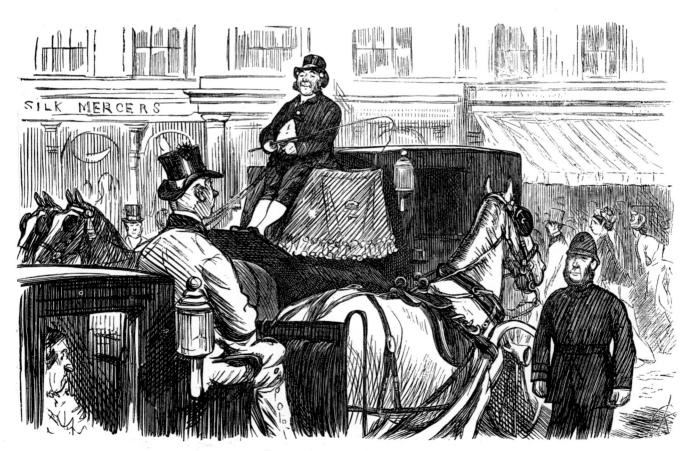

Punch

Punch

unch

Chinese porters with pedicab. *Peoples of the World*

Coachmen continued

Modern Pen Drawing

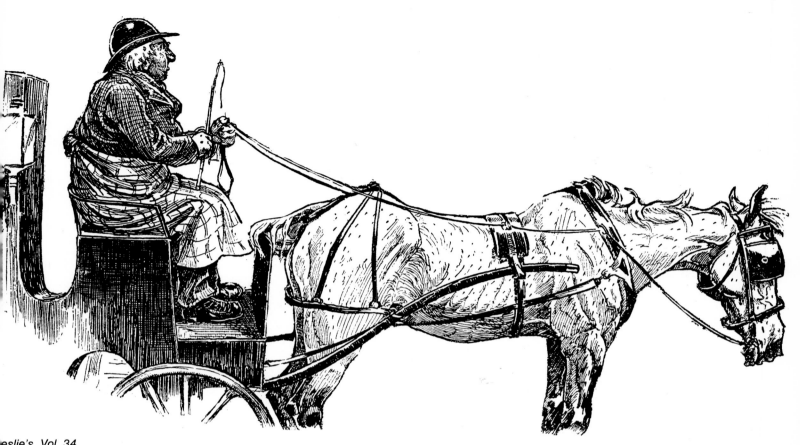

eslie's, Vol. 34

Coachmen continued

Coachman. *Century Magazine*

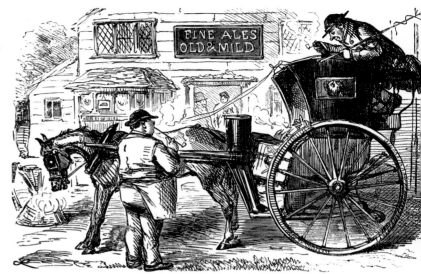

Punch

Punch

English hackney coachman of the time of Charles II. *Leslie's*

English Illustrated

English Illustrated

Punch

Punch

Coachmen continued

Judge

Punch

...rgotten Children's Books

Life

Female Approach

Cobblers

Modern Pen Drawing

Picture Book Of Graphic Art, Vol. 3

Comic Almanac

mplicissimus

Caricature and Comic Art

Medieval shoemaker's shop. *Leslie's*

Cobblers continued

History of Art □

Natural History

Leslie's

Roman cobbler. *Peoples of the World*

Harper's

A Jerusalem shoemaker's shop. *Picturesque Palestine*

Cobblers continued

Leslie's

Harper's

Leslie's □

ing room in a boot factory. *Harper's* □

Harper's

Construction Workers

Judge

Illustrated London News

Ancient Egyptian bricklayers. *Sunday Book*

Punch, Vol. 48

Construction Workers continued

Building the Thames embankment, London. *Illustrated London News*

French Advertising Art

French Advertising Art

...rt of the Book □

Caricature □

Lustige Blätter

Construction Workers continued

Graphics of Lvov

French Advertising Art

House construction, Fiji Islands. *Natural History*

Drawing by Grandville. *La Caricature* ◻

Natural History

Construction Workers continued

Modern Pen Drawing

Constructing a gate house in a New York aqueduct. *Harper's*

yaks raising a roof in Borneo. *Peoples of the World*

atural History

Japanese construction workers. *Harper's*

Construction Workers continued

French Advertising Art

Leslie's

History of the World, Vol. 1

French Advertising Art

Construction of the Paris Exhibition building. *Illustrated London News*

Harper's

Cowboys

The old trapper.
Century Magazine, Vol. 14

Cutting out a steer. *Century Magazine, Vol. 13*

A Texas cowboy.
Century Magazine, Vol. 14

Dissolute cow-punchers. *Century Magazine, Vol. 14*

Vaquero.
Century Dictionary

Saddling fresh horses. *Century Magazine, Vol. 13*

ucking bronco. *Century Magazine, Vol. 13*

Century, Vol. 13

Cowboys continued

The herd at night. *Century Magazine, Vol. 13*

Branding a calf. *Century Magazine, Vol. 13*

Brazilian cowboys using the lasso and bolas. *Harper's*

Chasing a calf. *Marvels of the New West*

Branding a horse. *Century Magazine, Vol. 13*

ording a deep river. *Century Magazine, Vol. 13*

The rope corral. *Century Magazine, Vol. 13*

Century Magazine, Vol. 13

Roping in a horse corral. *Century Magazine, Vol. 13*

Cowboys continued

Bronco busters saddling an untamed horse. *Century Magazine, Vol. 13*

Driving to the round-up. *Century Magazine, Vol. 13*

d-time mountain man with his ponies. *Harper's*

Century, Vol. 15

In a stampede. *Century Magazine, Vol. 13*

oping a steer. *Century Magazine, Vol. 13*

Cowboys continued

A fatal stampede. *Marvels of the New West*

Harper's

Around the campfire. *Century Magazine, Vol. 13*

ruising for missing stock. *Century Magazine, Vol. 13*

Trailing cattle. *Century Magazine, Vol. 13*

On A Mexican Mustang

Riding the line in winter. *Century Magazine, Vol. 13*

Cowboys continued

Throwing the lasso. *On A Mexican Mustang*

Sheep shearer. *Marvels of the New West*

Century Magazine, Vol. 14

An Arizona cowboy. *Century Magazine, Vol. 13*

anchero. *Century Dictionary*

The round-up. *Century Magazine, Vol. 13*

Criers

Harper's

Book of Days, Vol. 1

Gebrauchsgraphik

Modern Pen Drawing

English town crier. *Harper's*

Dancers

Drawing by Grandville. *Un Autre Monde*

Little Egypt and Anita. *Police Gazette, 1895*

Drawing and Design □

Police Gazette

Drawing by Grandville.
La Vie des Animaux

Drawing and Design □

Drawing by Grandville.
Un Autre Monde

Punch

Dancers continued

For Whom the Cloche Tolls

Harper's

Drawing and Design □

Daumier □

Caricature

Dancers continued

Daumier □

Caricature

Beardsley

dge

Beardsley

Caricature

French Ad Art

Dentists

Masterpieces

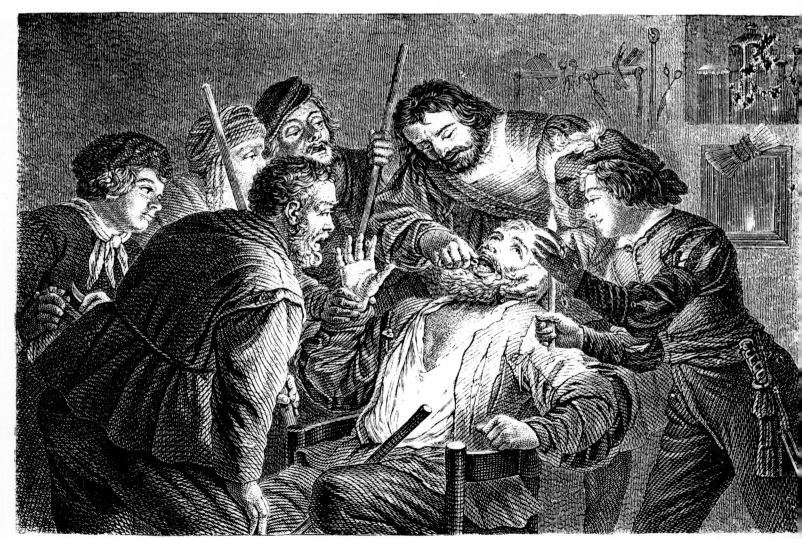

Masterpieces

Lustige Blätter

Masterpieces

Masterpieces

Dock Workers

Unloading a cargo of fruit at the wharf in Nassau. *Leslie's*

Storing coffee in a warehouse in New York. *Leslie's*

arper's

Illustrated London News

en and women unloading a steamer. *Harper's*

Punch

Dock Workers continued

Voyages and Travels

Leslie's

Harper's

Leslie's

Loading bananas at Port Antonio. *Leslie's*

Dock Workers continued

THE FAST COMMODIOUS CLIPPER SEA KING WILL SAIL FOR SAN FRANCISCO

slie's

Great Industry

Lumber wharf on the North Pacific Coast. *Countries of the World*

Factory Workers

Saw grinders at work. *Illustrated London News*

Fifty Years of Soviet Art □

Slicing and canning pineapple for export. *Leslie's*

Telegraph cable manufacturing. *Illustrated London News*

Factory Workers continued

Interior of a soap factory, Marseilles. *Harper's*

Harper's

Coral workers, Torre del Greco. *Leslie's*

Shoe-bottoming room in factory of B.F. Spinney & Co., Lynn, Massachusetts.

Indigo factory at Allahabad.

Factory Workers continued

Leslie's

Paper making. *Harper's*

The boring engine. *Harper's*

Stitching book bindings in a factory. *Harper's*

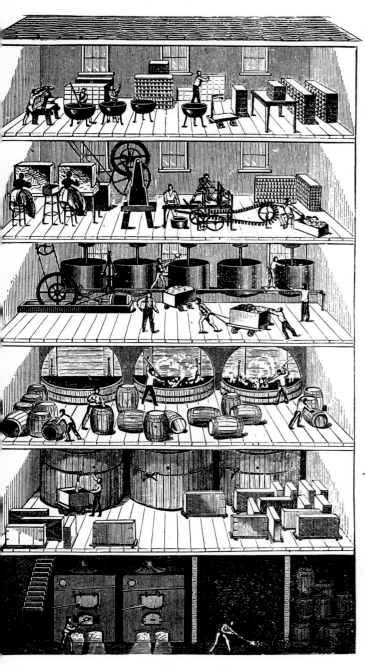

Grinding. *Harper's*

Packing chocolates in a candy factory. *Harper's* □

ap manufactory of E. Morgan's Sons. *Harper's*

Shirt cutter.
Century Magazine, Vol. 13

Harper's

Firemen

Fire in a New York theater. *Harper's*

Fire guard at the Academy of Music, New York.
Leslie's

Harper's

Peck's Compendium of Fun

iremen clearing a portion of ruins. *Illustrated London News*

Holiday exercises of the Japanese fire department. *Leslie's*

Fishermen

Lopmen on the Tarim. *Through Asia* □

Salmon-spearing on the Dee at Braemar, Scotland. *Leslie's*

Bartlett

Salmon fishing on the Columbia River. *Harper's*

ountries of the World

Gloucester fishermen. *Leslie's* □

atching lobsters. *Harper's*

Fishermen continued

Harper's

Arabian Nights

St. Nicholas

Sardine fishing. *Peoples of the World*

Fisher-folk at Mentone. *Peoples of the World*

Fishing during the Neolithic period. *Peoples of the World*

Harper's

Fishermen continued

Punch

Fishing in Norway. *Polar and Tropical Worlds*

ood Words

Sponge fishing along the Florida reef. *Harper's*

Fishermen continued

An eel fisherman. *Leslie's*

Natural History

Harper's

Natives fishing with a net. *Natural History*

Picture Book of Graphic Arts, Vol. 3

shing for tunny at Madrigue on the coast of Province. *Ocean World*

Fishing scene on the Andaman Islands. *Natural History*

Fishermen continued

Ocean World

Africans fishing. *Natural History*

Dressing down the catch. *Harper's*

Harper's

kagen fisher-girls. *Harper's*

Fishing in the Indian Ocean. *Ocean World*

Fishermen continued

Hauling in the lines. *Illustrated London News*

Norman fisher-girl. *Zigzag Journeys*

Fishing with bows and arrows. *Peoples of the World*

inese fisherman. *Natural History*

Bartlett

Indians fishing in the Alleghany River. *Leslie's*

Fishermen continued

Village of Fishtown during the business season. *Leslie's*

Fifty Years of Soviet Art □

arper's

Tagging salmon. *Harper's*

Dalmatian sponge fishermen. *Natural History*

Fishermen continued

Picturesque Palestine

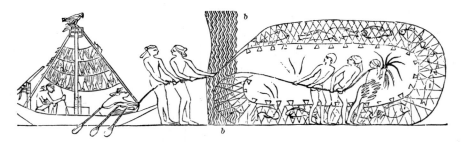

Ancient Egyptian fishing scene. *Zell's*

Oyster gathering. *Harper's*

unting herds on the sea. *Leslie's*

epairing the nets. *Harper's*

Shark fishing. *Harper's*

Fishermen continued

Fishing for crabs. *Harper's* □

Harper's

Catching and boxing crabs. *Leslie's*

...cient Egyptian fishermen with nets.
...*l's*

Weighing the catch for market. *Leslie's*

...arl fishing near Loch Lubnaig, Perthshire. *Illustrated London News*

Fishermen continued

Fisherman and his net. *Sunday Book*

Fishermen on the Sea of Galilee. *Picturesque Palestine*

...hermen of the west coast of India. *Natural History*

Early Advertising Art

...aring salmon by torchlight. *Leslie's*

Herders

Peoples of the World □

Early Illustrators

Herdsmen on the military confines. *Peoples of the World*

Countries of the World

Art of the Book

Herders continued

Art in 1898 □

Herdsmen and poulterers treating sick animals. *Harper's*

Catchpenny Prints

eep rancher. *Marvels of the New West*

eep herding at the ruins of the Samaritan Temple, Mount Gerizim. *Picturesque Palestine, Vol. 1*

Herders continued

Art of the Book

Harper's

Art of the Book □

At the brook, from a painting by Heinrich Johann Zugel. *Masterpieces in German Art*

per's

Harper's

Herders continued

Harper's

Albanian shepherd. *Peoples of the World*

Druse shepherd.
Century Magazine, Vol. 13

On A Mexican Mustang

Returning from the Commons, from a painting by Eugene Verboeckhoven. *Masterpieces in German Art*

Lambing time. *Leslie's, Vol. 24*

ghis shepherds. *Century Magazine, Vol. 14*

Herders continued

Driving sheep near Leenane, Ireland. *Leslie's, Vol. 11*

Famous Paintings □

...eoples of the World

...aphics of Lvov

Aldine

Hunters

Pigeon-catching. *Natural History*

Scandinavian hunter. *Historians' History*

Gebrauchsgraphik

Harper's

A French-Canadian trapper. *Century Magazine, Vol. 14* □

Harper's □

...e hunter and his day's provisions. *Natural History*

Aldine

...e moose at bay. *Harper's* □

Harper's

Hunters continued

Californians lassoing a bear. *History of the United States*

Modern Woodcuts

Moose hunting on the Yukon River. *Harper's*

Forgotten Children's Books

Shooting pigeons on the Têche. *Leslie's*

reindeer hunt during the Paleolithic epoch.
oples of the World

St. Nicholas □

Hunters continued

Through the Woods

Harper's □

Native archer. *Natural History*

Bringing home the deer. *Harper's*

Giraffes in a pitfall. *Natural History*

arper's □

Quaint Cuts

Duck hunter. *Leslie's*

Iron Workers

Scythe grinders. *Illustrated London News*

Natives smelting iron. *Harper's*

Finishing a newly forged machine part. *Leslie's*

arper's

Picture Book of Graphic Arts, Vol. 3

Dumping iron ore and coal into the blast furnace. *Choice Reading*

Iron Workers continued

Founder's shop during the Bronze Age. *Peoples of the World*

Primitive furnace for smelting iron. *Peoples of the World*

Picture Book of Graphic Arts, Vol. 3

Discharging the furnaces. *Harper's*

ddler converting pig iron into wrought iron.
arper's

The forges in an iron works. *Choice Reading*

Iron Workers continued

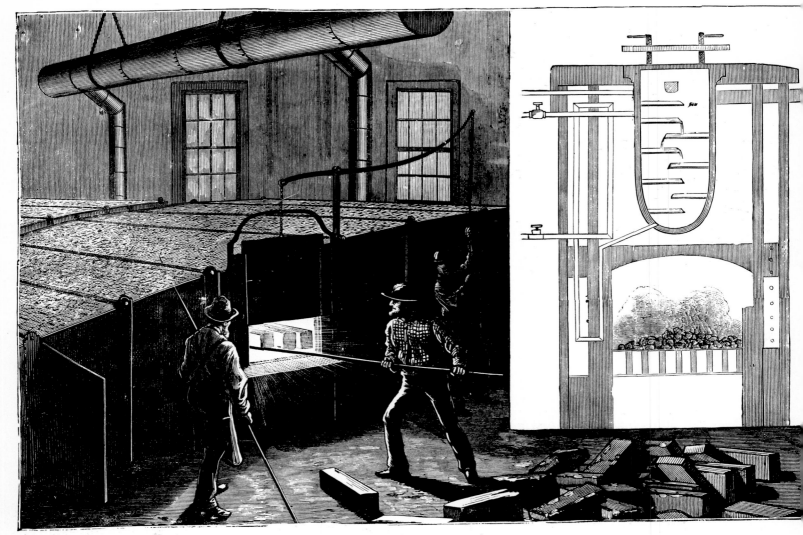

Manufacturing iron by the petroleum process. *Illustrated London News*

Heating furnace and a nail-making machine. *Harper's*

Molten metal running into pig molds.
Choice Reading

terior of a blast furnace. *Harper's*

Cutting metal plates. *Harper's*

able knife grinders. *Illustrated London News*

Iron Workers continued

Swedish peasants dredging for lake iron ore. *Peoples of the World*

Modern Pen Drawing

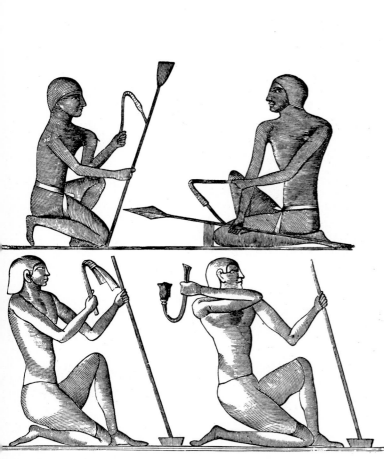

ncient Egyptians forging spears. *Sunday Book*

Scribner's □

rawing and Design □

Lawyers & Judges

Good Things

Bab Ballads

Leslie's

Drawing by Honoré Daumier. *Daumier Album.* □

Leslie's

Daumier

Harper's

Deutsches Lachen

Lawyers & Judges continued

Judge □

French Ad Art

Punch

Police Gazette, 1883

Harper's

Daumier

Lawyers & Judges continued

Daumier

London Illustrated News

Judge

Punch

Lawyers & Judges continued

Consulting the lawyer. *Leslie's*

Lawyer, by E.W. Kemble.
Century

Drawing by Honoré Daumier. *Daumier Album.* □

Cranford

he Court of Assizes. *Strand*

Bab Ballads

Froissart's Modern Chronicles

Punch, Vol. 29

Leather Workers

Beaming hides for leather manufacture. *Leslie's*

Tannery workers in Santo Domingo. *Leslie's*

...kers in a Leather factory. *Leslie's*

...s drying outside a tannery. *Harper's*

Handling small skins in a Leather factory. *Leslie's*

Loggers

Sawing trees into logs. *Harper's*

History of Art

Fifty Years of Soviet Art

Leighton □

Loggers continued

Driving the logs down river. *Harper's*

Harper's

Harper's

Harper's

Illustrated London News

Cutting the big pines. *Countries of the World*

Cutting and hauling wood. *Harper's*

Loggers continued

Modern Pen Drawing

Leighton □

oggers. *St. Nicholas*

Great Industry

Loggers continued

Lumbering in the Washington Territory. *Harper's*

Harper's □

Graphics of Lvov

Harper's

Harper's

Loggers continued

Graphics of Lvov

Early Illustrators

Harper's

Leslie's

Early Illustrators

Harper's

Loggers continued

Harper's

Felling trees in Lebanon. *Sunday Book*

Loggers breaking up a jam. *Harper's*

Graphics of Lvov

Harper's

arper's

Graphics of Lvov

Loggers continued

Graphics of Lvov

Illustrated London News

Reuben Davidger

Leslie's

...tives felling timber. *Indika*

Loggers at Puget Sound, Washington. *Harper's* □

Miners

Coaling in Seattle. *Harper's*

Blasting in the lower mine. *Harper's*

The affusto and perforators. *Harper's*

Harper's

The diamond diggings in South Africa. *Leslie's*

Miners continued

Gold washing in the Sierra Nevada. *Voyages and Travels*

Hydraulic mining. *Harper's*

Miners working a quicksilver machine. *Harper's*

Clearing a tunnel. *Harper's*

New Woodcuts

Miners continued

Miners at the phosphate diggings near Charleston. *Leslie's*

Tunnel mining at Table Mountain. *Harper's*

Harper's

The heading. *Harper's*

ound sluicing. *Harper's*

Mining. *Harper's, 1857*

Miners continued

Cut in a Georgia gold mine. *Leslie's*

Placer mining. *Marvels of the New West*

Interior of a mine. *Harper's*

Miners in Colorado. *Voyages and Travels*

Winnowing gold. *Harper's*

Miners continued

Fifty Years of Soviet Art ☐

Harper's Roundtable □

alian miner. *Harper's*

Drifting and shaft-sinking. *Marvels of the New West*

ushing an ore cart. *Harper's*

Stratification of coal beds. *Before the Deluge*

Miners continued

Interior of a salt mine. *Harper's*

Harper's

Harper's

Washing for gold. *Marvels of the New West*

oping. *Marvels of the New West*

Harper's

epairs after a mine explosion. *Illustrated London News*

Musicians

Peoples of the World

Bizarre

Harper's

Painting found in a tomb at Thebes. *Harper's*

Gebrauchgraphik, No. 12

Mark Twain's Library of Humor

Minstrel. *Illustrated London News*

Musicians continued

Female Approach

Punch, Vol. 12

Gebrauchsgraphik

Harper's

Roman horn players. *Classic Myths*

Caruso □

Punch, Vol. 23

The piper. *Harper's*

Playing an ancient drum. *Antique Musical Instruments*

Musicians continued

Tambourine. *Antique Musical Instruments*

Ox horn blower. *Sunday Book*

Gebrauchsgraphik

Servians guitarists. *Leslie's*

...et musicians. *Harper's*

Gebrauchsgraphik

Punch

Punch

Tavern musician. *Illustrated London News*

Harper's

Musicians continued

A Burmese band. *Peoples of the World*

Art Nouveau

Harper's

Comic Almanac

Female Approach

wing by Grandville. *Un Autre Monde* □

Life

Gebrauchsgraphik

Turkoman musicians. *Peoples of the World*

Musicians continued

Masterpieces

Beardsley

Judge

Caricature

Daumier □

Musicians continued

Fandango at the village. *Harper's*

Art of the Book □

Daumier □

Musicians continued

Harper's, Vol. 50

The anvil chorus. *Harper's*

Punch

Accordion player. *Century*

An Indian harlequin playing the part of a tiger. *London Illustrated News*

Flowers of Happiness

Musicians continued

A troubador. *Leslie's*

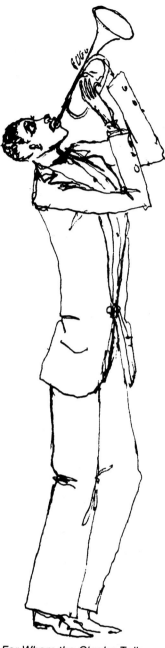

For Whom the Cloche Tolls

Decorative Silhouettes

nging men of Syria. *Sunday Book*

Bab Ballads

Comic Almanac

Musicians continued

Drawing and Design ◻

Gebrauchsgraphik

Quaint Cuts

Sang, a Chinese
musical instrument.
Century Dictionary

Grandfather's Moneybox

Roumanian gypsy musicians at the Paris Exposition. *Leslie's*

Musicians continued

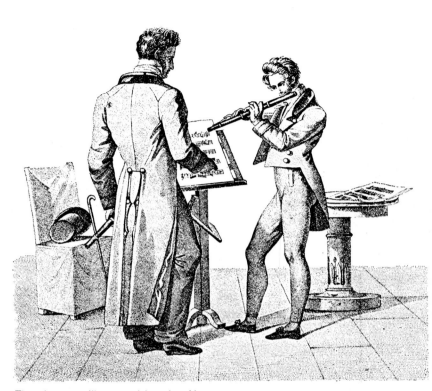

Flute lesson. *Illustrated London News*

Ballerina, after an etching from Jacques Caillot's "I Balli di Sfessania," 1602. *Plays, Players, & Playwrights*

A Soudanese orchestra. *Leslie's*

Quaint Cuts

Drawing by Grandville. *Petites Misères*

oples of the World

Punch

Musicians continued

Graphics of Lvov

Russian musicians. *Leslie's*

Harper's

Peck's Compendium of Fun

Chinese Cutout

The traveling musicians. *Harper's*

Catchpenny Prints

Punch

Musicians continued

Punch

Wilhelm Butch Album

Notes of a Collector □

Drawing and Design □

Book of Days, Vol. 2

The cornet player takes a bow.
Harper's, Vol. 8

Gebrauchsgraphik

Lady with a lute. *Century Magazine*

Harper's

Harper's

Youth's Companion

Newsboys

New York. *Life* □

Harper's

Century Magazine

Century Magazine, Vol. 15

Century

Nuns

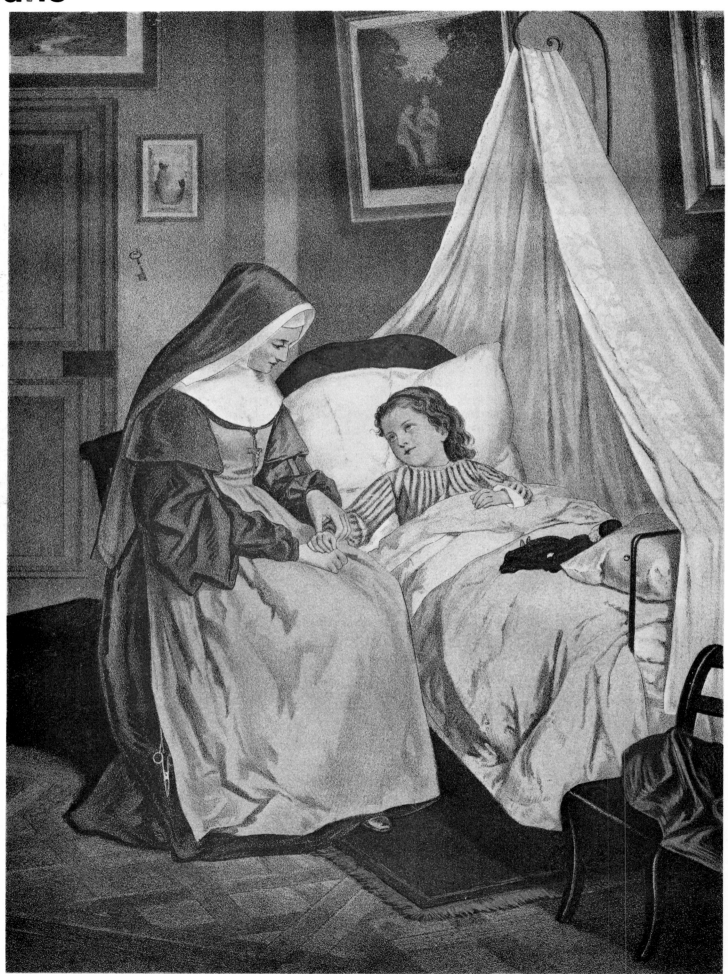

Leslie's □

arper's □

Leslie's

The Sisters at recreation. *Century*

Nuns continued

The walk at St. Anne's. *Century*

Hungarian nun. *People's of the World*

Scribner's

Modern Woodcuts

y Years of Soviet Art □

Century

rper's, Vol. 30

Essays on Polish Graphic Arts □

Nurses

Leslie's

House and Home

the surgical ward. *House and Home*

Harper's, Vol. 57

Famous Paintings

Peddlers

Hawaiian poi dealer. *Harper's*

Harper's

Peoples of the World

Harper's

The costermonger. *Leslie's*

Peddlers continued

Catchpenny Prints

Hay peddler. *Harper's*

Flower sellers in the Golden Temple. *Harper's* □

Street vender. Historian's History

garian fruit merchant. *Peoples of the World*

Punch

Drawing by Grandville. *Un Autre Monde*

Peddlers continued

Apple seller.
Peoples of the World

A market scene in Bethlehem. *Modern Pen Drawing*

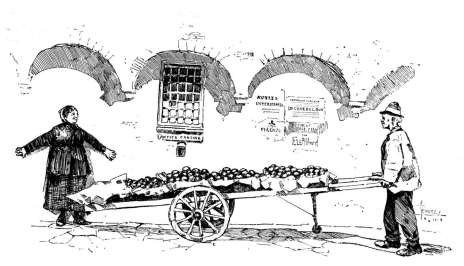

Leslie's

Chestnut vendor. *Leslie's*

er's

The toy peddler. *Modern Pen Drawing*

ch gypsy. *Peoples of the World*

Indian pottery vendors. *Leslie's*

Peddlers continued

German flower-women. *Leslie's*

Fruit sellers outside the mosque at Nazareth. *Picturesque Palestine*

Punch

Poi seller. *Leslie's*

Japanese salt vendor. *Leslie's*

Costermonger of Naples. *Peoples of the World*

Peddlers continued

Chinese fruit seller. *Peoples of the World*

Forgotten Children's Books

Thomas Hood

Bird dealer. *Peoples of the World*

Forgotten Children's Books

Drawing by Grandville. *Les Français Peints pars Aux-mêmes*

Punch

Harper's, Vol. 46

Matches for sale. *Forgotten Children's Books*

Peddlers continued

The basket seller. *Harper's* □

Harper's

Leslie's

Harper's

Harper's

he cats' meat man. *Leslie's*

Harper's

Flower seller. *Graphics of Lvov*

Peddlers continued

Sherbet seller in Cairo. *Illustrated London News*

Spanish street peddler. *Harper's*

The peacock seller. *Good Words*

Zulu women selling pumpkins. *Peoples of the World*

Photographers

Police Gazette

Harper's

Comic Almanac

Harper's

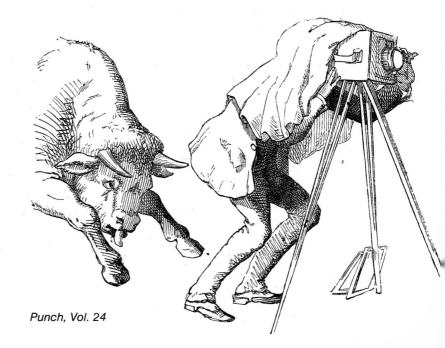

Punch, Vol. 24

Punch

Niepce de St. Victor taking photographs of French soldiers. *Leslie's*

Physicians

Judge

Modern Pen Drawing □

Judge

Physicians continued

Receiving patients in the examination room. *Harper's*

Female Approach

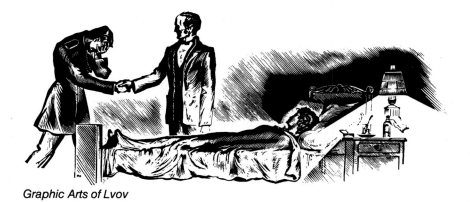

Graphic Arts of Lvov

Reducing a luxated shoulder. *Zell's*

Mark Twain's Library of Humor

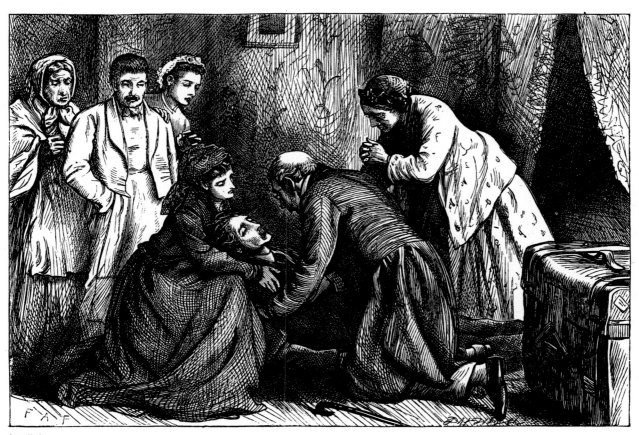

Leslie's

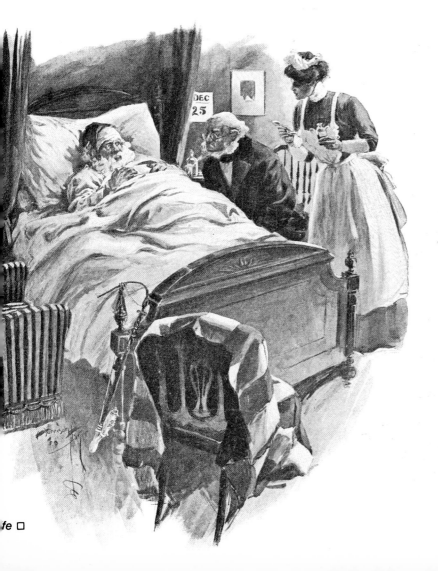

fe ☐

Dr. Quackenboss. *Harper's*

Physicians

Harper's

Punch

A physician of the East. *Sunday Book*

Rabelais

Gulliver's Travels

Female Approach

Treating a fractured leg. *Harper's*

Punch

Doctor. *Leslie's*

Policemen

Bab Ballads

Punch

New York Police Department patrol wagon. *Harper's*

St. Nicholas

Punch, 1879

Wilhelm Butch Album

St. Nicholas

New York policeman of 1693. *Harper's*

Scratchboard Drawing

Punch

Century Magazine

Policemen continued

Turkish police. *Riverside Natural History*

Harper's

Quaint Cuts

Punch, 1876

Harper's, Vol. 47

Punch

Strand Magazine

ceman of the Broadway squad. *Harper's*

Female Approach

Munsey's Magazine

Policemen continued

Arresting a thief at the Grand Central depot. *Harper's*

Punch, 1870

Harper's

Police Gazette

Caricature

Caricature

Postmen

Forgotten Children's Books □

Harper's

Harper's

Fifty Years of Soviet Art

post station on the great Siberian road. *Century Magazine, Vol. 14*

Postmen continued

A post station on the Barnaul road. *Century Magazine, Vol. 14*

Harper's

Departure of the mail wagon. *Century Magazine, Vol. 14*

Harper's

Art in 1898 □

Printers

Harper's

Pulling a proof of an engraved block. *Harper's*

Harper's

...ravers. *Leslie's*

Art of the Book

...engraving department. *Leslie's*

Printers continued

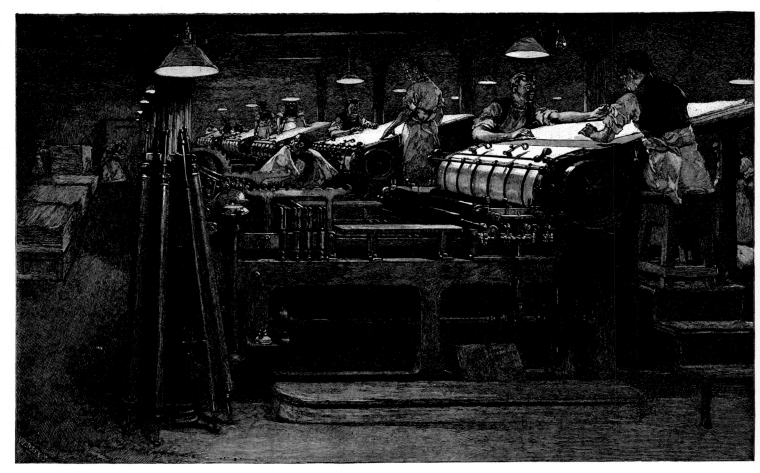

Press room workers. *Harper's*

Franklin's printing press. *Harper's*

Faust's first proof from moveable type. *Harper's*

The press room. *Leslie's*

ving and Design ☐

A compositor at work. *Harper's*

Quarriers

Harper's

Great Industry

Centennial Exposition

untries of the World

Harper's

per's

Harper's

Railroad Workers

The conductor. *Harper's*

The switch-tender. *Harper's*

Fifty Years of Soviet Art □

kmen. *Illustrated London News*

The brakeman. *Harper's*

The engineer. *Harper's* □

Railroad Workers continued

Working the interlocking switches. *Harper's*

Century Magazine, Vol. 15 ☐

The signal-box at London Bridge station. *Illustrated London News*

The signal-man. *Harper's*

king the engine. *Harper's*

The fireman. *Harper's*

Sailors

Harper's Roundtable □

Leslie's

St. Nicholas

Harper's

...pman in his canoe. *Through Asia* □

Art of the Book □

Robinson Crusoe

Sunday Book

Century Magazine, Vol. 13

Sailors continued

*Around the World
Through Arctics and Tropics*

Century Magazine, Vol. 13 □

Harper's

Harper's

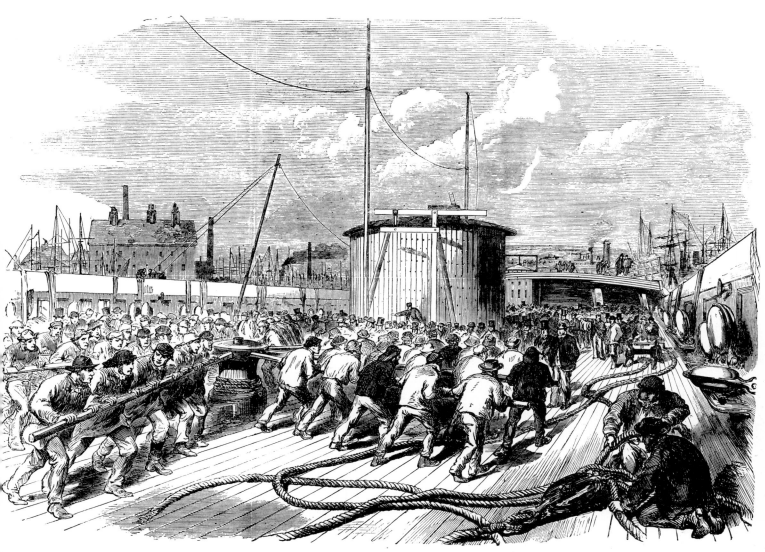

Illustrated London News

Old Engravings

lie's

Sailors continued

Russian boatman.
Nadir Abdurakhmanov

Source Illustrations

Harper's

Harper's Vol. 68

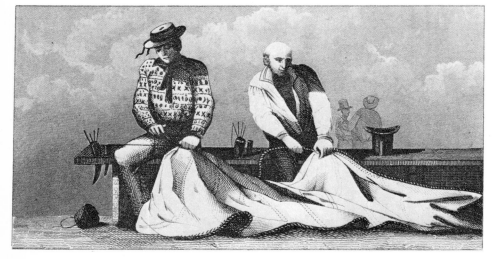

Harper's □

Century Magazine

Leslie's

Volga boatmen. *Nikolai Ivanovich Piskarev* □

aphics of Lvov

Sailors continued

Launching the lifeboat. *Leslie's*

Perfect Jewels

Harper's

unding the abyss with piano wire. *Century Magazine, Vol. 16*

Leslie's

Harper's

Sailors continued

St. Nicholas

Good Words

Source Illustrations □

Harper's □

arper's □

Nicholas

Sailors continued

Illustrated London News

Fifty Years of Soviet Art

Dutch boatman.
The World: Its Cities and Peoples

Harper's Roundtable

Servants

Punch, Vol. 26

Harper's

Masterpieces in German Art

Egyptian maid servants. *Sunday Book*

Drawing by E.A. Abbey, 1884. *Century Magazine*

Comic Almanac

Servants continued

Lithograph by Emanuel Wyttenbach.

Masterpieces in German Art

Harper's

Century Magazine

Servants continued

Drawing by Aubrey Beardsley. *Collected Drawings*

Masterpieces in German Art

Punch, Vol. 26

Punch

Servants continued

Punch

Harper's

Punch

Century Magazine, Vol. 15

Egyptian man servant. *Sunday Book*

Harper's

Caricature and Comic Art

Harper's

Shopkeepers

Drawing by Grandville. *Petites Miseres*

Scribner's

Punch

Cheese seller. *Harper's*

Carpet merchants. *Century Magazine, Vol. 15*

...icature

Harper's, Vol. 2

Shopkeepers continued

Punch

Shopkeeper at Bona. *Choice Reading*

Vegetable dealers at the French Market, Louisiana.
Century Magazine, Vol. 13

Grocer's shop in Jerusalem. *Picturesque Palestine*

Shopkeepers continued

Punch

Good Things

Japanese butcher's shop. *Leslie's*

Butcher, by E.W. Kemble. *St. Nicholas*

Rice dealers in Patna, Behar Province. *Peoples of the World*

A curiosity stall in Rome. *Harper's*

Singers

Punch

Drawing & Design

Rabelais

Bizarre

Deutsches Lachen

Punch

Bizarre

Rabelais

Tailors

Century Magazine,
Vol. 15

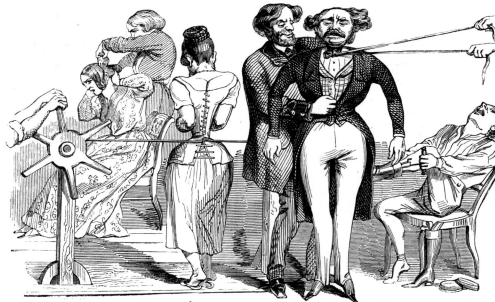

Drawing by Grandville. *Petites Misères*

Leslie's

Harper's

Fifty Years of Soviet Art □

rper's

Harper's

Tailors continued

Art of the Book

Tailors. *Century Magazine*

Hindu tailors and seamsters. *Leslie's*

storians' History

bute Book

Police Gazette ☐

Tailors continued

Peoples of the World

Peoples of the World

Life

Illustrated London News

Scratchboard Drawing

Japanese tailor. *Leslie's*

Teachers

Caricature

Punch, Vol. 25

Harper's

Harper's

Century

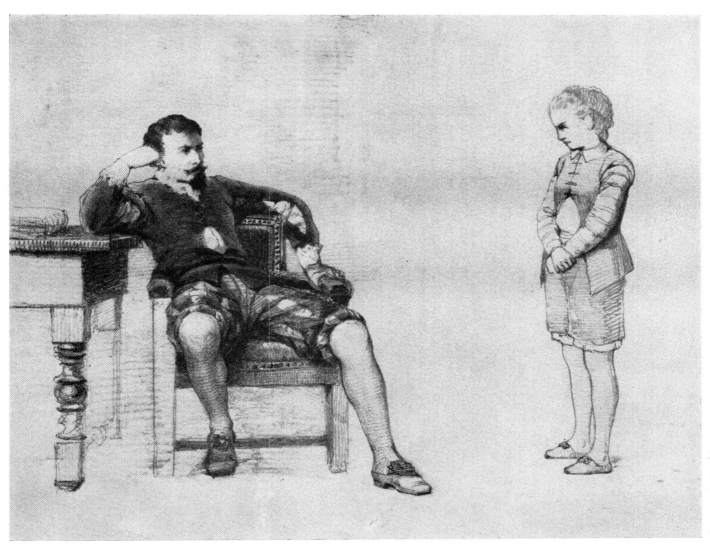

Fifty Years of Soviet Art □

nch

Harper's

Teachers continued

Century □

Punch

Lustige Blätter

Drawing by Hugh Thomson. *Our Village*

Reading lesson. *Harper's*

The arithmetic lesson. *Leslie's* □

Teachers continued

Life

Rabelais

Harper's

Century

Life

Youth's Companion

Professor. Leslie's

Teachers continued

There was a teacher named Bass
Who was really a silly old a

Jumbo Entertainer

Leslie's

Harper's, Vol. 58

Modern Pen Drawing

Bundle of Sunshine

Strand □

ood Things

Best Riddles

Teachers continued

Harper's

Harper's

Strand

Fifty Years of Soviet Art ☐

Quaint Cuts

Harper's

Punch

Tobacco Workers

A tobacco sale in New Orleans. *Leslie's*

Sealing tobacco cans. *Leslie's*

Flavoring the tobacco. *Leslie's*

owering canned tobacco into the boiler. *Leslie's*

Tobacco Workers continued

Sorting tobacco leaves for fillers. *Leslie's*

Spinning tobacco to make plugs. *Leslie's*

Tobacco plantation workers. *Leslie's*

Rolling in plug. *Leslie's*

eighing the tobacco cans. *Leslie's*

Steaming the tobacco. *Leslie's*

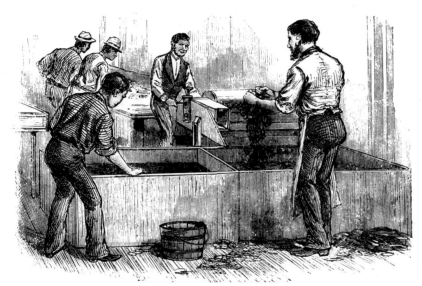

Drying tobacco leaves. *Leslie's*

e second drying process. *Leslie's*

Stemming tobacco leaves. *Harper's*

Vintners

Filling the beer kegs. *Harper's*

Crushing grapes for wine.
Bible Encyclopedia.

Wallachians distilling plum brandy. *Peoples of the World*

Inside a large beer brewery. *Leslie's*

oiling the beer. *Harper's*

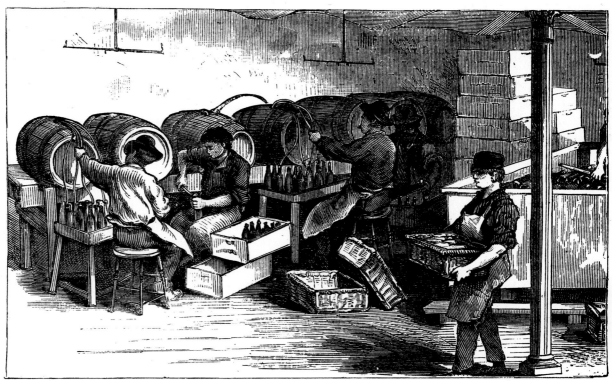

A peach brandy still. *Harper's*

e malting floor of a beer brewery. *Harper's*

Waiters & Bartenders

Harper's

Drawing by Aubrey Beardsley. *Collected Drawings*

Caricature

Leslie's, Vol. 35

Caricature □

Tea in the garden. *Harper's, Vol. 69*

Waiters & Bartenders continued

Waitresses with bloomers attract customers in San Francisco restaurant. *Police Gazette*

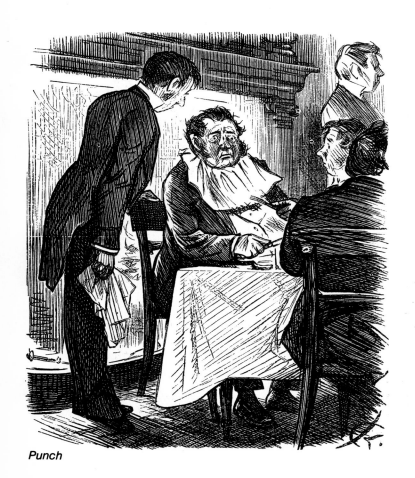

Punch

Punch, 1870

Graphic Trade Symbols

udge

Ruthless Rhymes

Waiters & Bartenders continued

Leslie's

The ale-wife. *History of Art*

Bartender. *On a Mexican Mustang*

Punch, Vol. 48

Punch, 1870

Wilhelm Butch Album

Harper's

Punch, 1870

Waiters & Bartenders continued

A gentleman at his club. *Punch, Vol. 29*

Caricature □

Fliegende Blätter

A Flemish citizen at meals.
History of Furniture

Punch

Waiters & Bartenders continued

Harper's Roundtable □

Punch

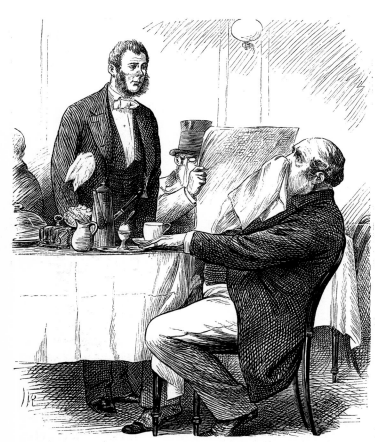

Punch

Caricature

d Things

Punch

Harper's, Vol. 50

Punch

Water Carriers

Picturesque Palestine

Sunday Book

Leslie's

Graphics of Lvov

Water Carriers continued

Riverside Natural History

Life of Greeks and Romans

Sunday Book

Peoples of the World

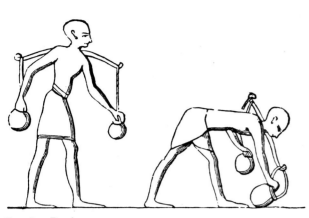

Sunday Book

Peoples of the World

arper's

Peoples of the World

Water Carriers continued

Peoples of the World

Life of Greeks and Romans

Picturesque Palestine

Harper's

Water Carriers continued

Leslie's

Good Words

Harper's

...erside Natural History

Harper's

Werbezeichen

Peoples of the World

Weavers

Art of the Book

Iberian weaver and spinner. *Peoples of the World*

Harper's

Native women weaving mats. *Natural History*

Masterpieces

Sorting cocoons of the silkworm. *Harper's*

aking the warp. *Harper's*

English Illustrated

Weavers continued

Oriental weaving. *Sunday Book*

Native women making cloth. *Natural History*

Harper's

Catchpenny Prints

Century Magazine, Vol.-15

Bowing cotton to remove seeds. *Picturesque Palestine*

Weavers continued

A jacquard loom. *Harper's*

Graphics of Lvov

Peoples of the World

Belkin's Stories

pinning and carding wool. Harper's

French Ad Art

Writers & Scribes

Public scribe. *The Aldine*

Strand

Fifty Years of Soviet Art

Taking pen in hand. *Nikolai Ivanovich Piskarev*

Strand

The Arab scribe. *Harper's*

Writers & Scribes continued

A Tunisian letter-writer. *Leslie's*

Samantha at the World's Fair

Harper's

Harper's

Beardsley

Writers & Scribes continued

A scribe. *Fifty Years of Soviet Art* □

Caricature □

Pickwick Papers

Art of the Book

Graphics of Lvov

Art of the Book

Strand

The near-sighted reporter. Strand

St. Nicholas

SOURCES

SOURCES

AL'BINA MAKURAITE. Korsakaite, Ingrida. Moscow: Soviet Artist (Sovetskii Khudozhnik), 1972.

ALDINE, THE: full title, *The Aldine, A Typographical Art Journal.* New York: James Sutton & Company, vol. 5, 1873.

ALEKSANDR VASIN. Bubnova, Ludmila. Moscow: Soviet Artist (Sovetskii Khudozhnik), 1972.

ANTIQUE MUSICAL INSTRUMENTS; full title, *Antique Musical Instruments and Their Players (Gabinetto Armonico).* Bonanni, Filippo. New York: Dover Publications, Inc., 1964. (From plates which first appeared in Rome, 1723).

ART IN 1898; full title, *A Record of Art in 1898.* London: The Studio, no date.

ART NOUVEAU: full title, *Art Nouveau, An Anthology of Design and Illustration from the Studio.* Gillon, Edmund V., Jr., ed. New York: Dover Publications, Inc., 1969.

ART OF THE BOOK, THE (fourth edition). Moscow: 1967.

ART OF THE BOOK, THE (seventh edition). Moscow: 1971.

ART OF THE SILHOUETTE, THE. Artists of the R.S.F.S.R. Leningrad: 1970.

BAB BALLADS, THE: full title, *The Bab Ballads, Much Sound and Little Sense.* Gilbert, W.S. London: George Routledge & Sons, no date.

BEST RIDDLES. Thompson, Jeff E. New York: Hart Publishing Company, Inc., 1957.

BIZARRE; full title, *Bizarre and Other Stories.* Mackall, Lawton. New York: Lieber & Lewis, 1922.

BOOK OF DAYS, THE (two vol). Chambers, R., ed. London: W.R. Chambers, 1864.

BUNDLE OF SUNSHINE, A. Woodruff, Press. Chicago: Monarch Book Company, 1901.

CARICATURE: full title, *Caricature: Wit and Humor of a Nation in Picture, Song, and Story.* New York: Leslie-Judge Company, no date.

CARUSO; full title, *Caricatures by Caruso.* Sisca, Michael. New York: La Follia Di New York, 1939.

CATCHPENNY PRINTS; full title, *Catchpenny Prints: 163 Popular Engravings from the Eighteenth Century.* New York: Dover Publications, Inc., 1970.

COUNTRIES OF THE WORLD, THE. Brown, Robert. London: Cassell and Company, Limited, no date.

CENTURY DICTIONARY; full title, *The Century Dictionary and Cyclopedia* (twelve vol.). New York: The Century Company, 1889-1913.

CENTURY MAGAZINE; full title, *The Century Illustrated Monthly Magazine.* New York: The Century Company, vol. 1, 6, 8, 38; individual issues 1883, 1884, 1885, 1888, 1889, 1890, 1891, 1892, 1894, 1895, 1896, 1901.

CHINESE CUTOUT. Available from China Books and Periodicals, 125 Fifth Avenue, New York, N.Y.

CLASSIC MYTHS; full title, *The Classic Myths in Literature and Art.* Gayley, Charles Mills. Boston: Ginn & Company, 1893.

COLLECTED DRAWINGS; full title, *The Collected Drawings of Aubrey Beardsley.* New York: Bounty books, 1967.

COMIC ALMANAC, THE. Thackeray, Albert Smith, Gilbert A. Beckett, The Brothers Mayhew. London: Chatto & Windus, second series, 1844-1853.

CENTENNIAL EXPOSITION, THE. Ingram, J.S. Philadephia: Hubbard Bros., 1876.

CRANFORD. Mrs. Gaskell. Illustrated by Hugh Thompson. New York: Hart Publishing Company, Inc., 1976.

DAUMIER ALBUM. Wortmann, Wilhelm, ed. London: Nicholson & Watson, 1946.

DECORATIVE SILHOUETTES; full title, *Decorative Silhouettes of the Twenties for Designers and Craftsmen.* Day, Jo Anne C., ed. New York: Dover Publications, Inc., 1975.

DEUTSCHES LACHEN. Kehm, Hermann Siegfried. Leipsig: H. Fifentscher, no date.

DRAWING AND DESIGN; full title, *Drawing and Design, The Magazine of Taste.* New series I (May 1920), II (June 1920), III (July 1920), IV (August 1920), V (September 1920), VI (October 1920), VII (November 1920), VIII (December 1920), IX (January 1921), X (February 1921, XI (March 1921), XII (April 1921).

DROLL STORIES; full title, *Droll Stories Collected from the Abbeys of Touraine.* Balzac, Honore. London: Printed privately, no date.

EARLY ADVERTISING ART; full title, *The Handbook of Early Advertising Art.* Hornung, Clarence P. New York: Dover Publications, Inc., 1956.

ESSAYS ON POLISH GRAPHIC ARTS; full title, *Essays on Polish Graphic Arts of the First Half of the Twentieth Cen-*

tury. Tananaeva, Larisa Ivanovn Moscow: 1972.

FAMOUS PAINTINGS; full title, *Famo Paintings of the World.* New York: Fi Arts Publishing Company, 1895.

FEMALE APPROACH, THE. Sear Ronald. London: MacDonald Compar Ltd., 1950.

FIFTY YEARS OF SOVIET ART; full titl *Album: Fifty Years of Soviet A Graphic Arts.* Kupetsian, A., ed. Mo cow: Soviet Artist (Sovetskii Khudoz nik), no date.

FLIEGENDE BLATTER. Munich: Verl von Braun & Schneider, nos. 22(through 2292.

FLOWERS OF HAPPINESS; full tit *Flowers of Happiness for Belove Youth.* Witte, Albert, ed. Amsterdar Busy Bee Publishers, 1958.

FOR WHOM THE CLOCHE TOLLS. W son, Angus and Phillipe Jullian. Lo don: Methuen, 1953.

FRENCH ADVERTISING ART; full titl *Source Book of French Advertising A* London: Faber & Faber, 1970.

FROISSART'S MODERN CHRON CLES. Gould, Harruthers. London: Fisher Unwin., 1902.

GEBRAUCHSGRAPHIK. Holsche Eberhard, ed. International Advertisi Art, nos. 2, 9, 12, 16, (1956).

GOOD THINGS; full title, *The Goc Things of Life.* New York: Whit Stokes, & Allen, 1886.

GRANDFATHER'S MONEYBOX. Pe myak, Evg. Moscow: Young Guar 1972.

GRAPHIC ARTS OF LVOV. Kiev: Mist stvo, 1971.

GREAT INDUSTRY; full title, *T Great Industries of the United Stat* Greeley, Horace, et.al. Hartford: J Burr & Hyde, 1873.

GULLIVER'S TRAVELS; full titl *Gulliver's Travels into Several Rem Regions of the World.* Swift, Dean. Illu trated by T. Morten. London: Cass Petter, & Galpin, no date.

HARPER'S; full title, *Harper's Ne Monthly Magazine.* New York: Harp & Brothers, vol. 2, 3, 5, 8, 10, 16, 18, 20, 21, 30, 31, 32, 36, 37, 38, 41, 42, 43, 44, 46, 47, 48, 49, 50, 54, 66, 71, 88.

HARPER'S ROUNDTABLE. New Yo Harper & Brothers, 1896.

HISTORY OF THE WORLD; full ti *Historians' History of the Worl*

Williams, Henry Smith. New York: The Outlook Company, 1904.

JUDGE; full title, *Gems from Judge.* New York: Leslie-Judge Company, 1922.

JUMBO ENTERTAINER, THE. Hart, Harold, ed. New York: Hart Publishing Company, Inc., 1946.

LA VIE DES ANIMAUX; full title, *Scene de la Vie Privee et Publique des Animaux.* Grandville, J.J. Paris: Hetzel & Paulin, 1842.

LESLIE'S; full title, *Frank Leslie's Popular Monthly Magazine.* New York: Frank Leslie Publishing House, vol. 10, 12, 13, 14, 15, 16, 17, 21, 23, 24, 25, 26, 29, 31, 32, 34, 35, 36, 38.

LIFE; full title, *Life Magazine.* New York: Life Publishing Company, 1860.

LONDON ILLUSTRATED NEWS. London: George C. Leighton, vol. 48.

LUSTIGE BLATTER. Munich: no date.

MARK TWAIN'S LIBRARY OF HUMOR. Illustrated by E.W. Kemble. New York: Hart Publishing Company, Inc., 1975.

MASTERPIECES IN GERMAN ART, THE. Reed, Eugene J. Philadelphia: Gebbie & Company, no date.

MODERN PEN DRAWING; full title, *Modern Pen Drawing: European and American.* Holme, Charles, ed. London: The Studio, 1901.

MODERN WOODCUTS; full title, *Modern Woodcuts and Lithographs.* Holme, Geoffrey, ed. London: The Studio, no date.

NEW WOODCUTS, THE. Salaman, Malcolm C. London: The Studio, 1930.

NIKOLAI IVANOVICH PISKAREV. Garlenko, N.A. Moscow: Fine Arts (Izobrazitel'nye Iskysstva), 1972.

NOTES OF A COLLECTOR. Siderov,

Aleksei Alekseievich. Leningrad: Artist of the R.S.F.S.R. (Khudozhnik R.S.F.S.R.), 1969.

OUR VILLAGE. Mitford, Mary Russell. Illustrated by Hugh Thompson. New York: Macmillan & Company, 1893.

PEOPLES OF THE WORLD; see THE WORLD: ITS CITIES AND PEOPLE.

PECK'S COMPENDIUM OF FUN. Peck, W. George. New York: Manhattan Publishing Company, 1884.

PETITES MISERES; full title, *Petites Miseres de la Vie Humaine.* Grandville, J.J. and Old Nick. Paris: Fournier, 1843.

PICKWICK PAPERS, THE. Dickens, Charles. New York: Hart Publishing Company, Inc., 1976.

PICTURE BOOK OF THE GRAPHIC ARTS, 1500-1800. Hirth, Georg (compiled by). First Edition *(Kulturgeschichtliches Bilderbuch aus Drei Jahrhunderten),* Munich: Knorr and Hirth, 1882/90. Reissued 1972 by Benjamin Blom, Inc., New York. Vols. 1-6.

PLAYS, PLAYERS, & PLAYWRIGHTS; full title, *Plays, Players, & Playwrights: An Illustrated History of the Theatre.* Geisinger, Marion. New York: Hart Publishing Company, Inc., 1975.

POLICE GAZETTE, THE. Smith, Gene and Jayne Barry Smith. New York: Simon and Schuster, 1972.

PUNCH; full title, *Punch, or the London Charivari.* London: The Proprietors, vol. 12, 24, 25, 26, 29, 30, 31, 32, 48, 58, 59, 62, 70, 71, 72, 73.

QUAINT CUTS; full title, *Quaint Cuts in the Chap Book Style.* Crawhill, Joseph. New York: Dover Publications, Inc., 1974.

RABELAIS; full title, *The Works of Mr. Francis Rabelais.* Illustrated by W. Heath Robinson. London: Richard Clay & Sons, Ltd., no date.

ST. NICHOLAS; full title, *St. Nicholas Illustrated Magazine for Young Folks.* New York: The Century Company, 1887, 1888, 1889, 1908.

SAMANTHA AT THE WORLD'S FAIR. Josiah Allen's Wife (Holley, Marietta). New York: Funk & Wagnall's Company, 1893.

SCRIBNER'S; full title, *Scribner's Monthly, An Illustrated Magazine for the People.* Holland, J.G., ed. New York: Scribner & Company, vol. 3, 5, 20.

STRAND; full title, *The Strand Magazine.* London: George Newnes, Ltd., vol. 15.

SUNDAY BOOK, THE; full title, *The Pictorial Sunday Book.* Kitto, Dr. John, ed. London: The London Printing and Publishing Company, Ltd., no date.

WORLD: ITS CITIES AND PEOPLE, THE. Hodder, Edwin, M.F. Sweetser, Dr. Robert Brown. London: Cassell & Company, Ltd., no date.

THROUGH ASIA. Hedin, Sven. New York: Harper & Brothers, 1899.

UN AUTRE MONDE. Grandville, J.J. Paris: Fournier, 1844.

WILHELM BUTCH ALBUM. Butch, Wilhelm. New York: Frederick Ungar Publishing Company, no date.

WORKS OF RABELAIS, THE. London: Chatto & Windus, no date.

YOUTH'S COMPANION, THE. Boston: Perry Mason & Company, 1887.

ZELL'S; full title, *Zell's Encyclopedia and Atlas* (four vol.). Colange, Leo, ed. Philadelphia: T. Ellwood Zell, Davis, & Company, 1880.

INDEX

HART PICTURE ARCHIVES

COMPENDIUM

HUMOR, WIT, & FANTASY

THE ANIMAL KINGDOM

DINING & DRINKING

WEATHER

CHAIRS

JEWELRY

TRADES & PROFESSIONS

BORDERS & FRAMES

HOLIDAYS

WEAPONS & ARMOR

JARS, BOWLS, & VASES

TITLES IN PREPARATION

DESIGN MOTIFS

FACES

MERCHANDISE

SHIPS, SEAS, & SAILORS